Zhuangzi's Butterfly

Alice Brière-Haquet
Woodcut illustrations by Raphaële F...

(OH) EDITIONS

INTRODUCTION

Zhuangzi (late 4th century BC) was one of China's most significant proponents of Daoism. Daoism is an ancient philosophy that strives for harmony with nature, virtuousness and self-development. Zhuangzi's writings would later be hugely influential on Chan Buddhism.

Zhuangzi's story of the dreaming philosopher and the butterfly is meant to challenge us to think about one big question: how do we really know what's real? A dream feels real when we're in it, so how can we ever be sure that life isn't a dream? Or could it be that our dreams are, in fact, real, and "real life" is the dream? These are questions that have been debated for centuries, and arguably it's impossible to ever definitively answer them.

Zhuangzi dreams.

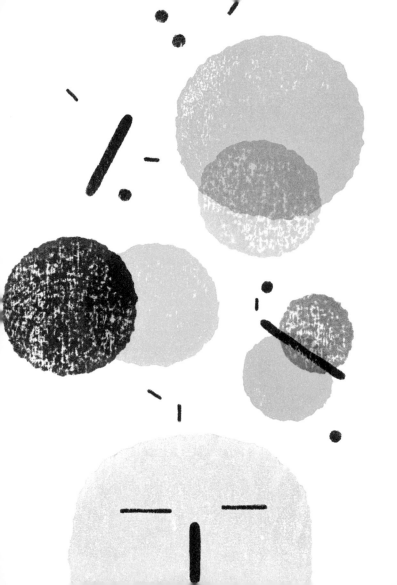

He dreams that he
has light wings...

He dreams that
he is a butterfly. What a
strange feeling!

He flutters in the wind,
from flower to flower,
happy just being himself.

Because the little animal
knows nothing about the man
who is dreaming.

So, when Zhuangzi wakes up,
when he finds his body,
sitting on the ground,
a thought occurs to him.

What if, at this moment,
it is the butterfly who is
dreaming of him?

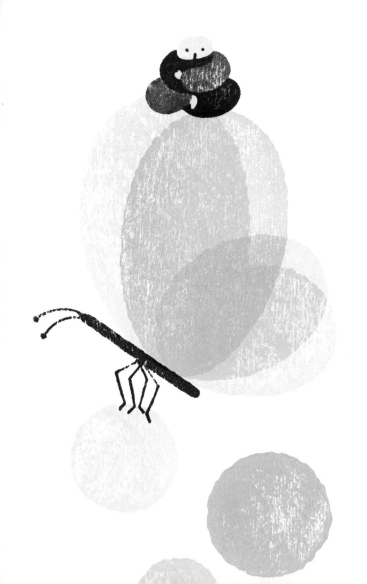

Who can tell…

Thoughts and reality are
such fragile things.

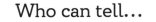